CAMELS
Ships of the Desert

CAMELS
Ships
of the Desert

By JOHN F. WATERS   Illustrated by REYNOLD RUFFINS

Thomas Y. Crowell Company   New York

LET'S-READ-AND-FIND-OUT SCIENCE BOOKS

Editors: **DR. ROMA GANS**, Professor Emeritus of Childhood Education, Teachers College, Columbia University
DR. FRANKLYN M. BRANLEY, Astronomer Emeritus and former Chairman of The American Museum–Hayden Planetarium

LIVING THINGS: PLANTS

Corn Is Maize: The Gift of the Indians

Down Come the Leaves

How a Seed Grows

Mushrooms and Molds

Plants in Winter

Roots Are Food Finders

Seeds by Wind and Water

The Sunlit Sea

A Tree Is a Plant

Water Plants

Where Does Your Garden Grow?

LIVING THINGS: ANIMALS, BIRDS, FISH, INSECTS, ETC.

Animals in Winter

Back Where They Came From: The Eels' Strange Journey

Bats in the Dark

Bees and Beelines

Big Tracks, Little Tracks

Birds at Night

Birds Eat and Eat and Eat

Bird Talk

The Blue Whale

Camels: Ships of the Desert

Cockroaches: Here, There, and Everywhere

Corals

Ducks Don't Get Wet

The Emperor Penguins

Fireflies in the Night

Giraffes at Home

Green Grass and White Milk

Green Turtle Mysteries

Hummingbirds in the Garden

Hungry Sharks

It's Nesting Time

Ladybug, Ladybug, Fly Away Home

The Long-Lost Coelacanth and Other Living Fossils

My Daddy Longlegs

My Visit to the Dinosaurs

Opossum

Sandpipers

Shells Are Skeletons

Shrimps

Spider Silk

Spring Peepers

Starfish

Twist, Wiggle, and Squirm: A Book About Earthworms

Watch Honeybees with Me

What I Like About Toads

Why Frogs Are Wet

THE HUMAN BODY

A Baby Starts to Grow

Before You Were a Baby

A Drop of Blood

Fat and Skinny

Find Out by Touching

Follow Your Nose

Hear Your Heart

How Many Teeth?

How You Talk

In the Night

Look at Your Eyes*

My Five Senses

My Hands

The Skeleton Inside You

Sleep Is for Everyone

Straight Hair, Curly Hair*

Use Your Brain

What Happens to a Hamburger

Your Skin and Mine*

And other books on AIR, WATER, AND WEATHER; THE EARTH AND ITS COMPOSITION; ASTRONOMY AND SPACE; and MATTER AND ENERGY

*Available in Spanish

Library of Congress Cataloging in Publication Data Waters, John Frederick, date Camels: ships of the desert. SUMMARY: Describes the physical characteristics of camels that enable them to withstand the heat of the desert for days at a time without water.
1. Camels—Juv. lit.   [1. Camels]   I. Ruffins, Reynold, illus.   II. Title.   QL737.U54W37   599'.736   73-14514
ISBN 0-690-00395-1 (lib. bdg.)

Ships
of the Desert

LET'S
READ
AND
FIND
OUT

Camels live where it is hot and dry. They live in the desert. People ride on camels. Camels carry heavy loads, too. They carry carpets and coconuts, dates and palm oil, salt, grains, all kinds of things. Camels are called "ships of the desert."

Did you ever walk in the sand? Did your feet sink down?

Camels can walk easily in the sand. They have wide, soft, padded feet that keep them from sinking into the sand or slipping on rocks.

Did sand or dirt ever blow into your eyes?
Camels have long, heavy eyelashes to help keep
sand out of their eyes.

Did sand or dust ever blow into your mouth, or
up your nose? Camels can close their nostrils.
Sand can't blow into their noses.

When you don't drink water for a few hours,
you get thirsty. Camels don't get thirsty that
quickly. In summer, when it is hot, camels can go
for eight days without a drink of water.

In winter some camels can go eight *weeks*
without a drink. They get the water they need by
eating juicy plants and bushes.

In very warm weather a man can live only two
or three days without water.

On a hot day in the desert, a rock in the sun
may reach 150 degrees Fahrenheit. If a camel
got that hot, it would probably die. So would you.
A camel keeps cool in the hot desert.

A camel sweats. That's one way it keeps cool. You keep cool that way, too. Sweating keeps your body temperature about 98.6 degrees Fahrenheit.

When you sweat, you lose water. If it's very hot and you sweat too much, you lose too much water. Then you must drink a lot.

On the desert in the early morning the camel's temperature is 93 degrees Fahrenheit. During the day the camel's temperature rises, but very slowly. It may be late afternoon before its temperature reaches 105 degrees Fahrenheit. Then it begins to sweat. At night the camel's temperature begins to drop down to 93 degrees again.